Contents

T0352009

Written by
Alison Hawes
Illustrated by
Stephen Elford

Series editor **Dee Reid**

Heinemann
Part of Pearson

Before reading *Freak!*

Characters

Tom

Sophie

Anna

Tricky words

- quiet
- confident
- laughed
- ignored
- corridor
- once
- gather
- chanted

Read these words to the student. Help then with these words whe they appear in the te

Introduction

Tom wasn't like any of the boys Sophie knew in Aspen Road School. He liked school and he was quiet but he also seemed confident. Sophie thought he was a freak and a wimp so one day she tried to get him into a fight.

Freak!

Tom wasn't like any of the boys Sophie knew in
Aspen Road School.
He didn't like football or computer games.
He liked school and books.
He was quiet but confident at the same time.
Sophie wasn't sure what to make of him.

She also didn't like the way he put his hand up in class all the time.

One day, when Tom had put his hand up for the fifth time, Sophie called out "Freak!"

Everyone laughed.

Everyone but Tom and Anna.

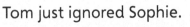

Tom just ignored Sophie.
But Anna turned to Sophie and said, "Take it from me, you don't want to mess with him."
But Sophie just laughed.

Later, in the corridor, Sophie and her mates blocked Tom and Anna's way.

"Excuse me, can we get past?" Tom said.

"Excuse me, can we get past?" Sophie mocked.
Tom ignored her and stepped to the side.
But Sophie didn't like being ignored.
"Wimp!" she said to his back.

Then one day, on the way home
from school, Sophie had an idea.
"Just watch this!" she said to her mates.

She ran up to Tom and bumped into him.
Then she let her school books fall in the mud.
"Hey freak!" she yelled, "Why don't you look
where you're going!"

"**You** bumped into me," said Tom. "Why don't **you** look where you are going!"
As Tom bent down to pick up Sophie's books she pushed him into the mud.
"Look at you, you freak!" she laughed.

Tom picked himself up and handed Sophie her books. For once, he looked cross.

"Fight! Fight!" Sophie's mates started to chant.
"Why don't you get lost!" said Tom.
But a crowd had started to gather.
"Fight! Fight!" they chanted, loudly.
"Wimp!" Sophie said.

Then she threw a punch.
In a flash Tom stepped to
the side and pushed her
hand away with the side
of his hand.
Sophie was so shocked she
didn't know what to say.

13

The crowd laughed when they saw
the look on Sophie's face.
She didn't like being laughed at.
She threw another punch.

Sophie wasn't sure what happened then.
But suddenly she couldn't move!
"Let me go!" she yelled.
"Go Tom! Go Tom!" the crowd chanted.
"The name calling stops NOW!" said Tom.
Sophie nodded and Tom let her go.

Anna went up to Sophie.
"I **told** you not to mess with him!" she said.
"Why didn't you tell me he was some
kind of kung fu freak," said Sophie.
"Just because he works hard at school
doesn't mean he's a wimp," said Anna.

Sophie looked at Anna.
She didn't like what Anna had said.
But she knew it was true.
"Whatever!" she said.

Quiz ////////////////

Text comprehension

Literal comprehension
p4 Why does Sophie get annoyed with Tom?
p15 Why did Anna tell Sophie not to mess with Tom?

Inferential comprehension
p7 Why does Tom not react to Sophie's name-calling?
p8 Why does Sophie try to provoke Tom?
p16 Why does Sophie say 'Whatever!' at the end?

Personal response
- Would you get annoyed with Tom?
- Do you think kung fu is as cool as football or computer games?

Word knowledge

p3 Which two words are contracted in 'wasn't'?
p8 Find two past tense 'ed' verbs.
p10 Why is the word 'You' in bold?

Spelling challenge

Read these words:

home began catch

Now try to spell them!

Ha! Ha! Ha!

What are the cleverest sweets?

Smarties!

Find out about

- the martial art of kung fu which is about learning self-defence.

Tricky words

- martial
- developed
- instructor
- taught
- peaceful
- self-confidence
- usually
- practising

Read these words to the student. Help ther with these words whe they appear in the te:

Introduction

Kung fu is a martial art of self-defence. It was developed in China hundreds of years ago. Kung fu became popular outside China after people saw the film 'Enter the Dragon' starring the Chinese American actor Bruce Lee.

Kung fu is a martial art.
It is about keeping fit and
learning to defend yourself.
Kung fu is **not** about learning to fight!

Like other martial arts, kung fu was developed in China hundreds of years ago.

Before the 1970s, not many people outside China knew about kung fu. Then in 1973, a film called 'Enter the Dragon' was made. The hero of the film was a Chinese American actor called Bruce Lee. He was also a martial arts instructor.

The film 'Enter the Dragon' and other kung fu films, made kung fu popular everywhere.
Now there are kung fu clubs all over the world.

There are many different styles of kung fu.
Bruce Lee was taught a style called
the wing chun style of kung fu.
But later, he developed his own style of
kung fu.

Wing chun kung fu was developed in China in the 1600s. People are often surprised when they learn that wing chun kung fu was developed by a woman!
She was a nun and a
martial arts instructor.
She thought people should
learn self-defence skills but
also live a peaceful way of life.

Wing chun is one of the best known styles of kung fu and is taught in many UK clubs today.

People learn kung fu for many reasons. Some people do it to keep fit or lose weight. Some people go to kung fu lessons to learn self-defence. Some people use it to improve their self-confidence.

What to wear

When you learn kung fu,
you need to wear loose-fitting clothes
like tracksuit trousers, a t-shirt and trainers.
If you get good at kung fu
you can wear a kung fu suit
and kung fu shoes.
A kung fu suit is usually a
black, loose-fitting top
and trousers. Kung fu shoes
are light and flat.

The space where you
learn kung fu is
called a kwoon.
Boys and girls train
together in the kwoon.
They learn the art of
self-defence.

Kung fu students must always show respect to their instructors.
They call their instructor 'sifu' which means master.
They must show respect to the other students too.

In their kung fu lessons, students learn
and practise different moves.
They learn to block, punch, kick and strike.
Sometimes they practise some moves on
their own.
Sometimes they practise with a partner.
Practising with a partner is called sparring.

When a student is learning the different moves of kung fu, the partner will hold a special pad and the student will punch or kick it.

Some moves in kung fu might look like fighting but kung fu is not the same as fighting. Kung fu students learn to respect and help their partner - not to hurt them.

Quiz //////////////////

Text comprehension

Literal comprehension
p20 Where was kung fu developed?
p21/22 What made kung fu popular all over the world?

Inferential comprehension
p24 Why might people be surprised to learn that wing chun kung fu was developed by a woman?
p29 Why must kung fu students show respect to their instructors?
p31 Why does a kung fu partner hold a special pad?

Personal response
- Have you ever tried kung fu?
- Why do you think it is such a popular martial art?

Word knowledge

p21 Why is 'Enter the Dragon' in inverted commas?
p24 Why is there an exclamation mark after the word 'woman'?
p26 Find a word that means 'to get better at something'.

Spelling challenge

Read these words:

before   which   high

Now try to spell them!

Ha! Ha! Ha!

What do martial arts instructors eat?

Kung food!